Acknowledgement of Land & of the Traditional Owners of this Land

I would like to acknowledge the Gadigal people of the Eora Nation, upon whose stolen land I stand on today.
I recognise that this land was never terra nullius — the land belonging to these peoples was never ceded, given up, bought or sold.
I would like to pay my respects to Aboriginal Elders past, present and emerging, and I extend this acknowledgement to all Aboriginal and Torres Strait Islander people.

Zombie

"Another head hangs lowly
Child is slowly taken
And the violence, caused such silence
Who are we mistaken?
But you see, it's not me
It's not my family

In your head, in your head, they are fighting
With their tanks, and their bombs
And their bombs, and their guns
In your head, in your head they are crying
In your head, in your head
Zombie, zombie, zombie-ie-ie
What's in your head, in your head
Zombie, zombie, zombie-ie-ie, oh

Another mother's breaking
Heart is taking over
When the violence causes silence
We must be mistaken

It's the same old theme
Since nineteen-sixteen
In your head, in your head, they're still fighting
With their tanks, and their bombs
And their bombs, and their guns
In your head, in your head, they are dying

In your head, in your head
Zombie, zombie, zombie-ie-ie
What's in your head, in your head
Zombie, zombie, zombie-ie-ie."

Songwriter: Dolores Mary O'Riordan

CONTENTS

1: You Don't Get to Choose Who You're Gonna LO♥E
(Non Puoi Scegliere chi Amerai)
2: I've Got My Dick in Line
(Ho il Mio Cazzo in Fila)
3: LO♥E is Something Beautiful
(Don't turn it into Something Bad)
(L'AMORE è Qualcosa di Bello
(Non Trasformarlo in Qualcosa di Brutto))
4: I Always Thought She Would Choose Me!
(Ho Sempre Pensato che Avrebbe Scelto Me!)
5: That's How It Goes
(È Così che Va)
6: Fanfare for the Common Man
(Fanfara per l'Uomo Comune)
7: It's Outta My Hands
(È Fuori dalle Mie Mani)
8: Signs
(Segni)
9: It's the Fucking Wild West Out There!
(È il Fottuto Selvaggio Ovest là Fuori!)
10: The Book of Miriam
(Il Libro di Miriam)
11: The Ghost of Vito Radice
(Il Fantasma di Vito Radice)
12: Convergence (not Divergence)
(Convergenza (non Divergenza))
13: Crying
(Piangere)
14: Get Out of My Head!
(Esci dalla Mia Testa!)
15: Clothes Are the Root of All Evil
(I Vestiti sono la Radice di tutti i Mali)
16: Last Gasp from a Drowning Man
(Ultimo Sussulto di un Uomo che sta Annegando)
17: Nobody Sings About How Greed Is Good
(Nessuno Canta di Quanto Sia Buona l'Avidità)

CONTENTS

18: Vito's "World Famous" Lentil Soup
(La Famosa Zuppa di Lenticchie di Vito)
19: Everything is Energy
(Tutto è Energia)
20: No One Will Corrupt Me
(Nessuno Mi Corromperà)
21: Interconnection
(Interconnessione)
22: All Is Fair (in LO♥E or war!)
(Tutto è Lecito (in amore o in guerra!))
23: To Work in a Bookshop (a job interview)
(Lavorare in Libreria (un intervista di lavoro))
24: I live in an asylum!
(Vivo in un Asilo!)
25: Ecstasy
(Estasi)
26: I Do Everything With LO♥E
(Faccio Tutto con AMORE)
27: Green Power
(Forza Verde)
28: Living Simply
(Vivere Semplicemente)
29: Simply Living
(Semplicemente Vivere)
30: Pagan Child
(Bambino Pagano)
31: This Could Be the Greatest LO♥E Affair in the Whole Universe
(Questa Potrebbe essere la più Grande Relazione d'Amore dell'intero Universo)
32: You've Gotta Find Your Own Voice
(Devi Trovare la tua Voce)
33: People Just Don't Like Their Lives
(Alla Gente Semplicemente non Piace la Loro Vita)

CONTENTS

34: Passengers
(Passeggeri)
35: Smoke & Lose Weight
(Fuma e Dimagrisci)
36: The Lightness of Being
(La Leggerezza dell'Essere)
37: Under the Southern Cross
(Sotto la Croce del Sud)
38: Letters to "The Don"
(Lettere a "Il Don")
39: The Big Sleep
(Il Grande Sonno)
40: Words Do Shit
(Le Parole Fanno Merda)
41: Green is the New Black
(Verde è il Nuovo Nero)
42: State of Desperation
(Stato di Disperazione)
43: Are You Judging Me?
(Mi Stai Giudicando?)
44: Poems Never Written (& other fragments)
(Poesie Mai Scritte (e altri frammenti))
45: Darkness at the Edge of Town
(Oscurità ai Margini della Città)
46: I'm Getting My Life Together
(Sto Mettendo Insieme la Mia Vita)
47: The End of Time
(La Fine dei Tempi)
48: Alive
(Viva)
49: The Youth Club
(Il Discoteca Giovanile)
50: Human Nature
(Natura Umana)

You Don't Get to Choose Who You're Gonna LO♥E
(Non Puoi Scegliere chi Amerai)

LO♥E finds you.
You have no control.
You have no say in it.
LO♥E just hits you.
Especially when you're not looking.
It just happens.
So don't fight.
Because...
...you don't get to choose who you you're gonna LO♥E.
You're just along for the ride.

Have faith!
Don't lose your faith.
You gotta trust LO♥E.
Believe in it.
Believe in it completely.
Let the Universe do its thing.
You have no control over this.
There is nothing you can do
You can't be proactive.
You can't plan.
Because...
...you don't get to choose who you you're gonna LO♥E.
You're just along for the ride.

LO♥E always wins.
That's what we live for.
LO♥E is the basis of everything.
LO♥E is life.
LO♥E is humanity.
LO♥E always comes through.
Because...
...you don't get to choose you you're gonna LO♥E.
LO♥E chooses YOU!
You're just along for the ride.

"The Don"
24.11.2021

I've Got My Dick in Line
(Ho il Mio Cazzo in Fila)

Yep...
...I'm standing here too.
I'm waiting here too.
I'm hoping that I get chosen.
I hope I'm next.
I've been here quite a long time.
But I don't care...
...*I've got my dick in line.*

I'm prepared to wait.
Stay as long as it takes.
I'm prepared to bide my time.
I'm ready to pay my dues.
I'm prepared for the hard yards.
It's OK...
...*I've got my dick in line.*

She is worth it.
She's the BEST!
She's got what it takes.
She's got it all.
She's *"top shelf"*.
She's *"hot shit"*
That's why...
...*I've got my dick in line.*

"The Don'"
25.11.2021

LO♥E is Something Beautiful
(Don't turn it into Something Bad)
(L'AMORE è Qualcosa di Bello (Non Trasformarlo in Qualcosa di Brutto))

Food...
...tick.
Work...
...tick.
Apartment...
...tick.
Friendship.
...tick.
Boyfriend...
...tick.
Sex...
...tick.
All boxes ticked.
The perfect life!

But...
...where is LO♥E?
LO♥E?
Yeah...
LO♥E?
I don't need it at the moment.
And anyway, LO♥E is too complicated.
But doesn't sex without LO♥E leave you empty?
Aren't you just using him?
And he's just using you.
You're just using each other.
I don't like the use of the word *"using"*?

Well, actually I think it's the BEST word to use.
It describes exactly what you are doing?
Because there is no LO♥E involved.
Sex without LO♥E is meaningless.
Sex with LO♥E is something beautiful.
Don't throw LO♥E away.
LO♥E includes the whole package...

...*food.*
...*work.*
...*apartment.*
...*friendship.*
...*boyfriend.*
...*sex.*
LO❤E is in everything you do.
LO❤E is not a bad thing.
LO❤E is something beautiful, don't turn it into something bad.

"That's how I LO❤E you."
"My LO❤E is all encompassing."
"That's what I give."
"It's your choice?"
"Emptiness or LO❤E?"
So, I say to you...
...*LO❤E is something beautiful, don't turn it into something bad.*

"The Don"
28.11.2021

I Always Thought She Would Choose Me!
(Ho Sempre Pensato che Avrebbe Scelto Me!)

I never doubted it.
I had faith.
I believed in LO♥E.
I believed LO♥E would win out on the end.
It didn't.
LO♥E lost.
Because...
...I always thought she would choose me!

She didn't.
She didn't choose me.
She chose someone else.
She didn't choose LO♥E.
LO♥E lost.
I Always believed LO♥E would win out in the end.
It didn't.
Because...
...I always thought she would choose me!

"And my HE♥RT is broken!"
"My HE♥RT is weeping!"
"My HE♥RT is bleeding!"
"I was delusional!"

"The Don"
29.11.2021

That's How It Goes
(È Così che Va)

It didn't work.
It didn't turn out as you would've liked.
You would've like it to have turned out differently.
But it didn't.
Just a accept it.
Because...
...that's how it goes.

Things didn't work out as you wanted.
You are disappointed.
You are sad.
You are depressed.
But you have to understood that sometimes...
...that's how it goes.

Don't be disappointed
Don't be sad.
Don't be depressed
Things didn't work out....
...this time!
Because sometimes...
...that's how it goes.

"The Don"
29.11.2021

Fanfare for the Common Man
(Fanfara per l'Uomo Comune)

Who stands up for the *poor?*
Who stands up for the *infirm?*
Who stands up for the *sick?*
Who stands up for the *unwanted?*
Who stands up for the *abandoned?*
Who stands up for the *rejected?*
Who stands up for the *dejected?*
Who stands up for the *abused?*
Who stands up for the *violated?*
Who stands up for the *discriminated?*
Who stands up for the *persecuted?*
Who stands up for the *disenfranchised?*
Who stands up for the *exploited?*
Who stands up for the *destitute?*
Who stands up for the *homeless?*
Who stands up for the *zombies?*
Who stands up for the *walking dead?*
Who champions their existence?
Who writes their story?
Who sings their song?
Where is...?
...the fanfare for the common man?
Who plays...?
...fanfare for the common man?

"The Don"
29.11.2021

It's Outta My Hands

(È Fuori dalle Mie Mani)

There is nothing I can do?
The die has been cast.
The outcome known.
The future has been written.
The words written in stone.
Blood is coming out of every letter.
The stone is crying.
It is crying because of the message it carries.
A burden it loathes to carry.
A message no one wants to see.
A message no one wants to read.
A message no eyes want look at.
Words no lips want to form.
Words no mouth wants to utter those words.
These words that can break stones.
These words that can break your bones.
These words that can blow your mind.
These words that can destroy your imagination.
These words that can turn your blood into rock.
These words that will tell you...
...that everything is outta your hands.

There is nothing you can do.
Because...
...everything is outta your hands.

"The Don"
29.11.201

Signs
(Segni)

Signs *everywhere.*
Signs *cluttering up the air.*
Signs *in your face.*
Signs *destroying the human race.*
Signs *in your mind.*
Signs *in front & behind you.*
Signs *all around you.*
Signs *all over the place.*
Signs *destroying the human race.*

Signs about *beauty.*
Signs about *survival.*
Signs about *hope.*
Signs about *faith.*
Signs about *belief.*
Signs about *truth.*
Signs about *happiness.*
Signs about *LO♥E.*

All these signs are *turning me blind.*
All these signs are *messing with my head.*
All these signs are *driving me mad.*
All these signs are *driving me crazy.*
All these signs are *making me insane.*
All these signs are *destroying me.*
All these signs are *destroying you.*

"The Don"
29.11.2021

It's the Fucking Wild West Out There!
(È il Fottuto Selvaggio Ovest là Fuori!)

Looters on the streets.
Boys carrying guns.
Lunatics shooting themselves...
...and anyone else who happens to unfortunately be there.
To use the old cliché...
...wrong place, wrong time.
It's a lawless jungle.
It's a war zone.
It's *"survival of the fittest"* out there.
It's the fucking "Wild West" out there!

Shops set on fire.
Buildings bombed.
Flags torched.
Effigies burnt to the ground.
Planes fly into multi-storey office buildings.
Suicide bomber blows himself to make a statement.
Gunman carries automatic shotgun...
...and kills 66 innocent children, women & men.
Why you might ask?
Because....
...it's the fucking "Wild West" out there!

"The Don"
29.11.2021

The Book of Miriam

(Il Libro di Miriam)

The *Book of Mariam* is closed.
The *Book of Mariam* is shut.
The *Book of Mariam* is locked.

The key to *The Book of Mariam's* lock is safely hidden away.
Engraved on the lock is...
...closed: 28.11 2021 @ 10:22pm.
Stardate: 74989.04
It is stored away in the "*Library of the Memory*".
High up on the very top shelf.
In the section called *"Lost LO♥ES"*.
Subsection, *"Lost Dreams"*.

"Goodbye & goodnight to The Book of Miriam."

"The Don"
29.11.2021

The Ghost of Vito Radice

(Il Fantasma di Vito Radice)

Who is *Vito Radice*?
What has he done?
What is his legacy?
Will anyone know who he was?
Will anyone remember him?
Will anyone really care?

What was he like?
As a person?
As a human being?
What did he say?
Did he say what needed to be said?
What did he do?
Did he do what needed to be done?
Was he a good & decent man?
Did he see wrong & try to right it?
Where there was suffering try to relieve it.
Where there was sadness bring happiness?
Where there was conflict try to resolve it.
Where there was hatred show how to LO♥E?
Where there was darkness bring in the light?

Where is he now?
Does anyone know?
Does anyone really care?
Probably not.
But the Universe remembers.
The Universe cares.
And that's good enough for him.
The ghost of Vito Radice is happy in this knowledge.
The ghost of Vito Radice can rest in peace.

"The Don"
30.11.2021

Convergence (not Divergence)

(Convergenza (non Divergenza))

Things are moving towards cohesion.
Events are coalescing.
The Universe is merging.
It's all about *"coming together"*.
It's all about achieving *"Oneness"*.
It's all about attaining *"Unity"*.
It's all about *"Singularity"*.
It's all about *"Entanglement"*.
It's all about coming to a *"Nexus"*.
It's all about *"Concentration of the Energy"*.
It's all about finding *"The Light"*.
It's all about manifesting *"The Force"*.
It's all about achieving *"Enlightenment"*.
It's all about coming to a *"Point"*.
It's all about reaching *"The Point of Origin"*.
It's all about achieving a *"Focal Point"*.
It's all about creating a *"Focus"*.
It's all about reaching the *"Epicentre"*.
It's all about *making LO♥E*.
It's all about *"Togetherness"*.
It's all about creating a *"Union"*.
It's all about *"Unification"*.
It's all about *"Convergence"*.
Follow the *"Path of Convergence"*.

*"He say I know you, you know me
One thing I can tell you is you got to be free
Come together, right now, over me"*

Songwriters: Lennon/Mccartney

"The Don"
30.11.2021

Crying
(Piangere)

Crying is such a weird thing
Why do we cry?
What causes it to happen?
Tears are such strange things.
Where do they come from?
What are they all about?
Tears coming out if your eyes.
Flowing down your cheeks.
Down onto your lips.
They taste salty.
What's this all about?
What's happening here?
Why do we cry?
What's its purpose?
What's it supposed to achieve?
I don't understand it?
I don't understand crying at all.

I know it's to do with sadness.
I know it's to do with emotions.
But what I don't understand are the tears coming out of our eyes.
What is that all about?
Why does this happen?
What are they supposed to do?
What...
...are they supposed to...
...wash all my sadness away?
...make everything better?
...make me feel better?
Crying is a weird thing!

"Anyway, I'm crying now!"
"Because I'm sad."
"My HE♥RT has been broken!"
"I have a broken HE♥RT!"
"So that's why I'm crying."
"But crying is still a weird thing that happens."

"The Don"
01.12.2021

Get Out of My Head!

(Esci dalla Mia Testa!)

Get outta my brain.
Get outta my mind.
You're driving me crazy.
You're driving me insane.
I can't get you outta my head.
Get outta my head.

I can't stop thinking about you.
I can stop thinking about all these different scenarios.
Creating scenes that never happened.
That never will happen.
My mind is in overdrive.
It can't stop.
I can't stop it.
I have no control over it.
I just want her to get out of my head.
Please...
...get out of my head.

"I'm going mad!"

"The Don"
01.12.2021

Clothes Are the Root of All Evil
(I Vestiti sono la Radice di tutti i Mali)

We should all be naked.
Throw our clothes away.
Stand completely nude.
Because when we wear clothes, we begin to have strange thoughts.
We start to do peculiar things.
We go all weird.
Clothes are the root of all evil.

Without clothes we would have nothing to hide.
We would be completely vulnerable.
Nothing to protect us.
Nothing to hide behind.
Nothing to conceal.
And no place to conceal it.
We would be totally vulnerable.
Clothes are used for use to hide in.
Both physically & mentally.
That's why...
...clothes are the root of all evil.

Once we started wearing clothes, the concept of *"concealment"* started.
To hide ourselves in.
To protect ourselves in.
This led to imagining what strange things lay hidden under those clothes that you are wearing.
I wanted to have a look.
I needed to see what was under your clothes.
I must get you to take your clothes off.
If you won't take them off voluntarily...
...then I will take them off you by force.
Can you see what has happened?
All because we started wearing clothes.
That's why...
...clothes are the root of all evil.

"Let's all take our clothes off & stand naked in front of the world!"
"Naked & proud!"
"Let's shout..."
"...I am naked & I am proud because I have nothing more to hide!"
This way clothes will no longer be the root of all evil.

"The Don"
01.12.2021

Last Gasp from a Drowning Man

(Ultimo Sussulto di un Uomo che sta Annegando)

It's so easy to *drown*.
It's so easy to *lose your life*.
It's so easy to *give up*.
It's so easy to *stop struggling*.
It's so easy to *die*.
It's so easy to take your last gasp.

I've become a *dead weight*.
I've become a *limp body*.
I've become a *lump of wood*.
I've become a *lifeless corpse*.
I've become a *drowning man*.

I have concrete feet.
I am sinking deeper.
I can see the sun shining though the water.
I am tired.
I stop struggling.
I take my last doomed gasp for air.
But it's not air...
...it's water.

Deeper & deeper I sink.
Darker & darker it becomes.
Until there is nothing.
Complete darkness.
The light in my eyes has disappeared.
The flame in my belly has gone out.
I am dead.

I close my eyes for the very last time.
I am dead.

"The Don"
01.12 2021

Nobody Sings About How Greed Is Good
(Nessuno Canta di Quanto Sia Buona l'Avidità)

Nobody writes songs praising *"Capitalism "*.
Nobody writes songs about how money made them happy.
Nobody writes about how money is good.
Nobody writes songs about how greedy they are.
Nobody Sings About How Greed Is Good

Nobody writes songs about how
they LO♥E being greedy!
Nobody writes songs about how being greedy is fantastic!
Nobody writes songs how they LO♥E money.
Nobody writes about how Greed is good.

Nobody sings songs praising *"Capitalism "*.
Nobody sings songs about how money made them happy.
Nobody sings about how money is good.
Nobody sings songs about how greedy they are.
Nobody sings songs about how they LO♥E being greedy!
Nobody sings songs about how being greedy is fantastic!
Nobody sings songs about how they LO♥E money.
Nobody sings about how Greed is good.

Nobody shouts out, *"I LO♥E being greedy!"*
Nobody shouts out, *"I am greedy & I am proud!"*
Nobody sings about how Greed is good.

"I wonder why?"

"The Don "
03.12.2021

Vito's "World Famous" Lentil Soup
(La Famosa Zuppa di Lenticchie di Vito)

Well, you might've come to the conclusion that Vito is a useless sod.
Good for northing!
Well, you're wrong!
He is good for something.
His "World Famous" lentil soup.

Have you tried it?
You don't know what your taste buds have missed out on.
Fernanda LO❤ES it!
And she knows her lentil soups!
She knows the difference between red, green & brown lentils.
Yes, there are 3 varieties.
Possibly even more!
Here is the recipe.
Follow these steps precisely.
Do not alter any.
Do not be creative.

Step 1:
To a large pot add...
...extra virgin olive oil *(preferably Italian)*.
...one large brown onion.
...plenty of garlic.
Fry until golden brown.
Do not burn!

Step 2: *(optional)*
Add...
...a can of diced tomatoes *(preferably Italian)*.
Fry for approximately 5 minutes.
Stir occasionally.
Do not burn!

Step 3:
Add approximately 2 cups of water.
(vegetable or chicken stock can be used instead)
Bring to the boil.
Stir occasionally.
Do not burn!

Step 4: *(optional)*
Add...
...diced carrots.
...diced potatoes.
Bring to the boil.
Stir occasionally.
Do not burn!

Step 5:
Lower temperature.
Let simmer for approximately 1 hour.
Stir occasionally.
If liquid is low, add water as required.
Do not burn!

Let cool.
Serve in a bowl with grated parmesan cheese sprinkled on top.

Enjoy!

Buon appetito!

"The Don"
03.12.2021

Everything is Energy

(Tutto è Energia)

Light is energy
Air is energy.
Music is energy
Our Thoughts are energy.
We are energy.
Communication is energy.
Human interaction is energy.
Your past is energy.
Your future is energy.
Your present is energy.
Everything is ENERGY!

Let's go deeper…
…deeper.

All your hopes are energy.
All your dreams are energy.
All your nightmares are energy
All your fears are energy.
All your rejections are energy.
All your relationships are energy.
All your LO♥ERS are energy.
All you LO♥E is energy.
All you HATE is energy.
Because…
…everything is ENERGY!

You are ENERGY!
I am ENERGY!

Everything is ENERGY!

"The Don"
03.12.202

No One Will Corrupt Me

(Nessuno Mi Corromperà)

They tried to *corrupt me*.
They tried to *buy me*.
They tried to *bully me*.
They tried to *abuse me*.
They tried to *vilified me*.
They tried to *destroy my reputation*.
They tried to *crucify me*.
I'm just glad they *didn't kill me*.
Because no one will corrupt me.

They tried to *make me think that I was crazy...*
...out of my thoughts.
Those deeply held thoughts...
...that you could not think!
The certainty of what is...
...of my beliefs.
...of myself.
...for me were NEVER questionable.
...NEVER in doubt!

How dare I have...
...thoughts that could not be thought.
...ideas that could not be held.
This could not be tolerated by the *"Suits"*.
The *"Men's Club"*.
They wanted me to join them.
They wanted me to join the *"Club"*.
But I had to lose...
...my principles.
...my ideals.
...my self-worth.
I had to become a man!

I chose not to.
I chose not to become one of them.
I chose not to be corrupted.
But no one will corrupt me.
NO ONE!

I cannot be bought!
I cannot be sold!
I am NOT a commodity!
I am NOT for sale!
At ANY price!
Because no one will corrupt me.

"The Don" + Miriam 06.12.2021

Interconnection

(Interconnessione)

Connecting.
Feeling.
Empathy.
Energy.
Space.
Time.
Space-Time.
It's all about interconnection.

Move out of your comfort zone.
Leave your bubble.
There is more to Heaven & Hell than you can ever imagine.
It'll blow your tiny little mind!
You think you're important?
You think you know everything?
You thing you're the centre of the Universe?
You're not important.
You know shit.
And you're not the centre of the Universe.
So...
...stop being a fucking arsehole.
It's not about you.
It's about interconnection.

Your *feelings.*
Your *thoughts.*
Your *imagination.*
Your *ideas.*
Your *energy.*
It's all about interconnection.

"The Don"
07.12.2021

All Is Fair (in LO♥E or war!)
(Tutto è Lecito (in amore o in guerra!))

All is fair...
...in LO♥E or war!
That's the rule.
Don't forget that.
Otherwise, you'll regret it.
And you'll be in deep shit.
Remember...
...all is fair...
...in LO♥E or war!

Don't *despair*.
Don't *freak out*.
Don't *become sad*.
Don't *get angry*.
Don't *hate*.
It won't do you any good.
Because...
All is fair...
...in LO♥E or war!

"The Don"
07.12.2021

To Work in a Bookshop (a job interview)
(Lavorare in Libreria (un intervista di lavoro))

*Thanks for your inquiry about work at "Hypatia Books".
I will be giving preference to people with bookshop experience (which this time around I have 3 apply so far).*

*If you are interested then the next step is to come in and sit the general knowledge book test which takes about 20 mins and have a brief informal chat with me.
You can't really prepare for the test as it is over lots of genres and is a bit random.
Most people have strength and weaknesses, so it tells me something about where they are for you as well as an idea as to how well read you are.
I formally interview on the results of the test (I'm looking for a 70%+ result before I interview).*

*To give you an idea of if it is worth both your time and ours to come in to do the actual test, we are including a MINI SELF TEST.
There is no room for bluffing, as the actual test is much longer and harder.
As a guide I would expect a result of at least 18/21 in the mini self-test for it to be worth considering having a go at the longer test.*

Name the author of the following books:

*The Hitchhikers Guide to the Galaxy
The Da Vinci Code
Cat's Eye
A Clockwork orange
In Cold Blood
The Cherry Orchard
The Alchemist
Disgrace
Little Dorrit
The Spy who came in from the Cold
Atonement
Lolita
Of Mice and men
A Room of One's own
Anna Karenina
Brideshead Revisited
Portrait of a Lady
The Great Gatsby
Sense and Sensibility
The Girl with the Dragon Tattoo
Oscar and Lucinda*

What is that all?

What about these questions....
What is...
...Einstein's famous equation relating energy & mass?
What is...
...Hawking's equation for determining the temperature of a black hole?
...who unified Italy & in what year?
...when was JFK killed, where & who was convicted?
...who wrote the song "Imagine"?

"I didn't realise I had to have a fucking photographic memory to work in a bookshop!"

My reply...

...Dear Melody,

Thank you for the opportunity to seek employment in your fantastic bookshop.

I did the mini quiz & my results are below.
My score was 16/21.

Would you still be interested in me even though I didn't achieve your minimum of 18/21.

As an addendum, I do have lots of personality, I live very close by & am an early riser.
If that is of any interest to you.

"I never got the job!"
"Fuck, I didn't even get an interview!"

"The Don"
08.12.2021

I live in an asylum!

We ALL live in an **asylum!**

It is called...

..."SOCIETY"!

"The Don'
08.12.2021

Ecstasy

(Estasi)

I saw it in your *face*.
I saw it in your *eyes*.
I saw it in your *body*.
I saw it in your *lips*.
Ecstasy.

I felt it in your *embrace*.
I felt it in your *body*.
I felt it in your *kiss*.
I felt it in your HE♥RT.
I felt it in your *soul*.
Ecstasy.

It *surrounded* you.
It *enveloped* you.
It *entered* you.
It *became one with* you.
It *changed* you
Ecstasy.

"The Don"
08.12.2021

I Do Everything With LO♥E
(Faccio Tutto con AMORE)

I open your bottle of beer with *LO♥E*.
I light your cigarette with *LO♥E*.
I play guitar for you with *LO♥E*.
I sing you songs with *LO♥E*.
I look at you with *LO♥E*.
I kiss you with *LO♥E*.
I do everything with LO♥E.

I would clean the floors for you with *LO♥E*.
I would walk 500 miles for you with *LO♥E*.
I would swim the English Channel for you with *LO♥E*.
I would dance the Tarantella for you with *LO♥E*.
I would stand naked in the snow for you with *LO♥E*.
Because...
...I do everything for you with LO♥E.
I do everything with LO♥E.

I will go to the end of the Earth for you with *LO♥E*.
I will do anything you want me to with *LO♥E*.
Because...
...I do everything with LO♥E.

"The Don"
08.12.2021

Green Power

(Forza Verde)

"Green power" is not new.
It's been here since the beginning of time.
It's the words of the Universe.
This is how it speaks.
It uses "Green Power".

"Green Power" is all around us.
It's in *everything*.
It's in the *air*.
It's in the *water*.
It's in the *rocks*.
It's in the *plants*.
It's in *animals*.
It's in *you*.
It's in *me*.
It's in *all of us*.
It's Nature.
It's "Green Power".

We have no choice about it.
There is no point running away from it.
There is no point denying it.
There's no point lying about it.
There's no point struggling with it.
There's no point fighting it.
Just recognise.
Just accept.
That we are ALL "Green Power".

"Green is the new Black!"
"Green Energy!"
"Green Power!"

"The Don"
10.12.2021

Living Simply

(Vivere Semplicemente)

Do you need all that stuff?
Do objects make you happy?
Do material possessions make you happy?
Does money bring you happiness?
Are you happy?
Try...
...living simply.

Declutter.
Give it away.
Throw them away.
Get rid of all that shit.
You don't need it.
It just causes misery.
It is hollow.
The answer is...
...living simply.

Material possessions only provide *"provisional happiness"*.
Material objects are just a *temporary fix*.
They only give you an immediate sense of happiness.
But it doesn't last long.
Then you need *another hit...*
...& another.
...& another.
...& another.
...& another.
You are now addicted.
Try something more long lasting & permanent.
Try...
...living simply.

"The Don"
11.12.2021

Simply Living

(Semplicemente Vivere)

It's not that difficult.
It's not that complicated.
We all know what to do...
...theoretically.
Deep inside.
When we stop for a moment & reflect…
…on our lives & it's direction.
And ask that eternal question...
..."*Am I happy?*"
It's all about *"simply living"*.

Simplicity is the key.
Simplicity is the answer.
Simplicity is the solution
Simplicity is the path to follow.
Simplicity is all that's required…
…to live a happy & meaningful life.
That's all.
That's...
...*simply living.*

Live simply.
Simply live.

"The Don"
11.12.2021

Pagan Child

(Bambino Pagano)

I'm a *"Pagan Child"*.
I see magic everywhere.
I see what others can't see.
Or don't want to.
I hear what others can't hear.
Or choose not to.
I do things that others don't.
Or can't.
I feel things others don't.
Or can't.
I imagine things others don't.
Or won't.
I create things others don't.
Or told not to.
I'm a *"Pagan Child"*.

I feel my HE♥RT.
I feel *Nature*.
I feel the *Universe*.
I am a *"Pagan Child"*.

I worship the Universe.
I worship the stars
I worship Nature.
I worship energy.
I do not worship false idols.
I do not worship false gods.
Because...
...I'm a *"Pagan Child"*.

Why don't you become one too?
Why don't you become a *"Pagan Child"*?
I'm a *"Pagan Child"*.

Why don't you become one too?
Why don't you become a *"Pagan Child"*?
I am a *"Pagan Child"*.

"The Don"
11.12.2021

This Could Be the Greatest LO♥E Affair in the Whole Universe

(Questa Potrebbe essere la più Grande Relazione d'Amore dell'intero Universo)

But it's not easy.
It doesn't happen overnight.
It takes time.
Lots of time.
And lots of hard work.
You can't be easily discouraged.
You have to stay focused.
You have to remind loyal.
No matter what happens.
No matter what the Universe throws your way.
Just jump over them
And continue on you path.
Because...
...this could be the greatest LO♥E Affair in the Whole Universe.

So, it's well worth it.
Don't give up.
Stick with it.
Because...
...this could be the greatest LO♥E Affair in the Whole Universe.

"The Don"
11.12.2021

You've Gotta Find Your Own Voice
(Devi Trovare la tua Voce)

It's hard to do.
It's better to *be someone else.*
It's better to *imitate someone else.*
It's better to *copy someone else.*
It's better to *hide behind a mask.*
It's harder to be yourself.
But you've gotta find your own voice.

You have to *stop faking it.*
You have to *throw all that baggage away.*
You have to *get rid of your burden that you carry on your shoulders...*
...that you carry in your head.
...that you carry in HE❤*RT.*
...that you carry in your soul.
...that you carry in your very Being.
You've gotta find your own voice.

Find yourself.
Go deep inside.
Look within.
That's where the answer lies.
Inside YOU!
And when you do…
… you will find your own voice.

Then…
…you don't need to force it.
…it happens naturally.
…without any effort.
…it is effortless.
…it is easy.
That's because...
…you have found your own voice!

"The Don"
11.12.2021

People Just Don't Like Their Lives
(Alla Gente Semplicemente non Piace la Loro Vita)

What a *shame*.
What a *pity*.
What a *disgrace*.
What a *travesty*.
What a *tragedy*.
What a *horror story*.
What a *nightmare*.
What a *LIFE*.
What a *DEATH*.

People just don't like their lives.
Don't be one of these people.

Otherwise, you will live your whole life...
...not liking your life.
...and not liking yourself!

So, don't be one of these people.
...people who just don't like their lives.

"The Don"
11.12.2021

Passengers

(Passeggeri)

We are not here to stay.
We are in transit.
This is not our final destination.
We are just visitors here.
We are just guests.
We are just passengers.

We cannot stay here forever.
Even if we wanted to.
We have no choice in the matter.
The decision was made for us.
We have no say in the situation.
We are just passengers.

There is no point *struggling against this.*
There is no point *fighting it.*
There is no point *being angry about it.*
There is no point *resisting it.*
Resistance is futile.
Because...
...we are just passengers.

We cannot *run away from this.*
We cannot *hide from this.*
We cannot *manipulate this.*
We cannot *buy our way out of this.*
We cannot *bribe our way out of this.*
Because...
...we are just passengers.

Jumping off is not an option either.
Acceptance is the only conclusion.
Our fate was determined a long time ago.
Even before we were born.
We were destined to be passengers.

So, sit back & enjoy the ride.
You can't get off.
No matter what you do.
No matter what you think.
No matter what you feel.
No matter what you imagine.
Because...
...we are just passengers.

So, it's very important to keep you cabin clean & tidy.
For the comfort of yourself & others.
Do not trash it.
Look after it.
Sit back...
...look out your window.
... and watch the world go by.
Because...
...we are just passengers.

We all just passengers.

"The Don"
12.12.2021

Smoke & Lose Weight

(Fuma e Dimagrisci)

Worried about your weight?
Worried that you've put on a few kilos?
Worried that you've gone up a couple of sizes?
Your pants don't fit you anymore.
You have to loosen your belt a couple of notches.
Or worse still...
...have to buy a new belt?
Don't worry I have the solution.
Smoke & lose weight.

Smoking makes you lose weight.
Yep...
...it's true.
Forget about your crash diets.
Just start smoking.
Smoke as much as you like.
Smoke everything.
Smoke anything.
Smoking doesn't kill.
Smoking makes you lose weight.

Wanna look trim, taut & terrific.
Smoke to your hearts delight.
Just Smoke your weight off.
Watch the kilos fall away with every puff…
…with every Smoke.
Delight yourself that with a smoke whenever & wherever you can.
Become a new you.
A new person.
Pretty soon you won't even recognise yourself.
You'll look at yourself in the mirror & say...
..."Who is that splendid example of a human being that I see looking back at me?"
That's what smoking can do for you!
So...
...smoke & lose weight.

"The Don"
12.12.2021

The Lightness of Being
(La Leggerezza dell'Essere)

Be *light*.
Be *weightless*.
Be *a butterfly*.
Be *the air*.
Be *a gentle breeze*.
Be *a whisper of music*.
Be *a gliding eagle*.
Be *a calm lake*.
Be *soft rays of sunlight in the evening*.
Be *caressing moonlight on a quiet night*.
Be *a soft kiss on your lips from your LO♥ER*.
Be *a warm cuddle from your pet dog*.
Be *the warmth from a burning log fire on a cold winter's night*.
Be *as light as a feather*.
Be *as fluffy as falling snow*.
Be *as spongy as lush green grass below my feet*.
Be *as happy as a laughing new born baby*.
Be *as free as rolling green meadows*.
Be *inspiring as the Grand Canyon*.
Be *as mesmerising as the stars up in the sky*.
Be *"The Lightness of Being"*.

"The Don"
12.12.2021

Under the Southern Cross

(Sotto la Croce del Sud)

The Southern Cross constellation.
4 stars in the shape of a cross.
A 5th pointer star inside.
Pointing to where?
To the centre of our galaxy...
...that beautiful spiral "Milky Way"?
And in its centre the sleeping monster called "Sagittarius A"...*
...a massive Black Hole.
...which one day, way into the future will destroy everything?
Maybe?

Our could it be closer to home?
Pointing here to Earth...
...our beautiful planet called "Terra"
And to particular position on this planet.
Pointing straight to our HE❤RTS?
Not just to one HE❤RT.
Not just to my HE❤RT.
But to ALL HE❤RTS.
And why the HE❤RT?
Is the HE❤RT so important?
The answer is right before your eyes.
Every night if you look up into the sky.
You will see the majestic Southern Cross constellation.
There is your answer.
That is your answer.
Your HE❤RT has spoken.
The Southern Cross has heard.

"The Don"
12.12.2021

Letters to "The Don"

(Lettere a "Il Don")

Have any issues that you need solved?
Have any problems that you need help with?
Want some advice on any issue?
"The Don" can help.
Write to *"The Don"*.
He will offer simple, clear & unbiased advice.
Completely objective & totally non-judgemental.
He will not disappoint.

"Dear Don"....

Dear Don,
I find that I am more and more attracted to barnyard animals as I get older. Is this wrong? And if not, which animal should I date first?
Signed Henderson Frawley
East Maitland.

Dear Henderson,
Thank for letter your & the issue that you have raised. Believe it or not you are not alone. There are many people who secretly suffer this very same situation. And is an issue that needs to be brought out into the open & not kept hidden in a barnyard.
There needs to be a national conversation about it.

Anyway, my advice to you is...
...start slowly & with inanimate objects first.
Try with something small first, such as a piece of fruit. My suggestion is to start with a rockmelon, it is small, easily fits in one hand & hold.
Become comfortable with this first & then move onto larger objects such as a watermelon.

The key here Henderson, is "baby steps".

Have fun & make sure to clean up afterwards.
"The Don"

Dear Don,
I'm at a nudist beach and I dropped my keys. Should I pick them up or should I catch a bus home?
Ainsley Dunbar,
Padstow NSW

Dear Ainsley,
Thank you for your very penetrative & probing question.
You are in luck my friend, for I am quite an expert on nudity & the necessary etiquette required to navigate the tricky minefield & potholes of a nudist beach.

My answer is... do not go completely "hello daisy" straight away. Check out the scene first & then gently ease yourself into the crouching position. Of course, if you feel perfectly comfortably, then I would have no problem with you bending over completely & picking up your keys.
My motto is... comfort first!
If you feel comfortable, bend over as far & as often as you like.

Happy foraging.
"The Don "

Dear Don,
My mum found some dirty pictures under my bed and now she says I'm going to hell.

Is this true?
John Jacobs
Castle Hill NSW

Dear John,
YEP! You are gonna burn in HELL!
And ALWAYS listen to your mother!
But now that you're going to HELL, you can do whatever the fuck you want.
ENJOY!
"The Don"

So, if you have any issues that you need help with, why not write to *"The Don"* & let him run his knowledgeable eyes over them?

Just mail them to, "Letters to *"The Don"*.
It doesn't matter where you are, everyone knows *"The Don"*!

"The Don" + Eric
14.12.2021

The Big Sleep

(Il Grande Sonno)

Wake up!
You've been asleep too long.
It's time to *arise*.
It's time to *get up*.
It's time to *start moving*.
It's time to awake from "The Big Sleeping".

There are *problems that need to be solved*.
There are *issues that need to be addressed*.
There are *crises that need to be confronted*.
Society is in chaos.
The Earth is being destroyed.
It needs your help.
So...
...you need to awaken from...
..."The Big Sleep".

You can't remain asleep forever.
You must awaken.
We need your voice.
We need you!
Please, awaken.
AWAKEN!
You MUST awaken from...
..."The Big Sleep"

Wake up!

"The Don"
14.12.2021

Words Do Shit

(Le Parole Fanno Merda)

Don't *talk*.
Don't *speak*.
Don't *say a fucking thing*.
Because...
.. *words do shit*.

Actions *count*.
Actions *mean something*.
Actions *are what's need*.
Because...
.. *words do shit*.

That's all that's *required*.
That's all that's *needed*.
That's all that's *necessary*.
Because...
.. *words do shit*.

Words are *cheap*.
Words are *plentiful*.
Words are *fake*.
Because...
...*words do shit*.

"Listen to my actions."
It's actions that speak.
Because...
.. *words do shit*.

"Actions speak louder than words."
Because...
.. *words do shit*.

"Words are cheap!"

"The Don"
16.12.2021

Green is the New Black

(*Verde è il Nuovo Nero*)

Green Power.
Green Energy
Green Planet.
Green Future.
Green Miriam.
Green is the new black.

Green thinking.
Green feeling.
Green living.
Green government.
Green society.
Green world.
Green is the new black.

Green Capitalism.
Green humans.
Green humanity.
Green LO♥E.
Green LIFE.
Green DEATH.
Green EVERYTHING.
Green is the new black.

Black is DEAD!
Green is the new black.

"The Don"
18.12.2021

State of Desperation

(Stato di Disperazione)

It's a State of *Annihilation*.
It's a State of *Desperation*.
It's a State of Destruction.
It's a State of *Suffocation*.
It's a State of *Dilapidation*.
It's a State of *Desecration*.
It's a State of *Californication*.
It's a State of *Confusion*.
It's a State of *Delusion*.
It's a State of *Execution*.
It's a State of *Illusion*.
It's a State of *Disillusion*.
It's a State of *Constrainment*.
It's a State of *Entitlement*.
It's a State of *Manipulation*.
It's a State of *Anxiety*
It's a State of *Darkness*.
It's a State of Desperation.

"We live in a State of Desperation!"

We live in a State of...

...*Ruination*,
...*Putrification*,
...*Unimaginative*,
...*Dissimulation*,
...*Inhabitation*,
...*Mortification*,
...*Suffocation*,
...*Subordination*,
...*Castration*,
...*Sublimation*,
...*Intoleration*.

We live in State of Desperation!

There is confusion all around.
Don't let desperation bring you down.
Just because we live in...
...State of Desperation!

Yep, we all live in a...
...State of Desperation.

A State of Desperation!

A State of Desperation!
Desperation.
Desperation.
We all live in a...
...State of Desperation!

A State of Desperation!

"The Don"
20.12.2021

Are You Judging Me?
(Mi Stai Giudicando?)

Don't judge *me*.
Don't judge *my decisions*.
Don't judge *my choices*.
Don't judge *my sex life*.
Don't judge *whom I fuck*.
Are you judging me?

Yes, I'm judging you.
We judge all the time.
We ALL judge.
Everyone judges.
You're judging me right now.
We have no choice.
That's what we do.
We judge.
Are you judging me?

Do you have an opinion?
"Yes, I have an opinion on everything!"
Having an opinion is judging.
"So, yes, I'm judging you".
"And you are judging me".
That's the way it is.
Are you judging me?

"So..."
"...if I agree with your point of view..."
"...I am not judging you."
"But..."
"...if I disagree with your point of view..."
"...I am judging you."

"Is that how it works?"
"Have I got it right?"

"So..."
"...what do you think?"
"Am I judging you?"
"Yes!"

"The Don"
19.12.2021

Poems Never Written (& other fragments)
(Poesie Mai Scritte (e altri frammenti))

She got a better offer.
If I had a conscience.
I never died.
New World rising.
Arse Licker!
Mother Fucker!
I don't need that shit!
We Are All Nothing.
We Are a cancer.
Be a teacher.
We wanna bring down the system.
We were all born to create.
From behind the wall.
What can I see?
Ayahausca.
I Think I'm in a Porno.
I see a girl I imagine her coming over to me & saying...
"...Wanna fuck?"
"And I say..."
"...Sure!"
The Outer Limits
Boyfriend...
...I'm your boyfriend.
What a weird representation.
What does that mean?
I'm you boyfriend.
Don't force.
Don't force anything that doesn't need to be forced.
(I've Got a) worried mind.
It's not what they say, but it's what they do that's important.
Don't be impressed with words.
...though eloquent they maybe.
...poetic even.
...definitely reassuring.
...very authoritarian, definitely.

But remember...
...it's not what they say but it's what they do that's important.
Keep Rolling.
Keep rolling.
Because...
...you're the rolling stone.

Reap what you sow.
Smoke blowing in the breeze.
That's all we are.
Gossamer whispers.
Fleeting whisps of cotton.
Shimmering currents of air.
A series of sin curves.
That's all we are...
...smoke blowing in the breeze.

Refraction of light.
A spectrum of rainbow colours.
Waves of gravity.
Cosmic winds.
The life force.
Maybe...
...even.
...life itself.
Because...
...that's all we are.
...smoke blowing in the breeze.
There's danger at the edge of town.

Talk, talk, talk.
Talk is cheap.
The glass is half full.
Can I make your garden grow?
My LO♥E for her is taking a long time to die.
You don't know the power of the pussy.
There are consequences for every action.
All I wanted was a little bit of LO♥E.

Thoughts of a poet.
But maybe one day....

"The Don"
21.12.2021

Darkness at the Edge of Town

(Oscurità ai Margini della Città)

There was darkness...
...at the far edge of town.
That's where we were at...
Maybe I'll never see her again
...at the far edge of town.
And this is destroying me.
I was too far gone.
There was no way for me to go back home.
But I'll be fine...
...one day.
Probably...
...not too far away.
I was nothing to her.
But you entered her...
...what was that like?

I was there when they crucified Jesus Christ.
I saw him suffer on the cross.
I offered up my hand.
He said *"Thanks but I have to suffer this alone."*
"There is nothing you can do for me."
"This is my moment."
"I have to do this alone."
"There is nothing you can do for me."
"It is written in the stars."
"This is my fate."
"I must suffer alone."
And with his last dying breath he said,
"I see all the madness in this world but there is nothing I can do about it!"
"That is why I'm being crucified!"
"Lord, have mercy on my soul!"
"Because I have failed."
"Let all the people weep."
"Let all the people cry."
"My life has been in vain."
"But at least I tried!"

"But don't worry..."
"...she never really LO♥ED you!"
I gave it my best shot.
I made sure there was nothing left in the tank.
Now, there is darkness at the edge of town.

"The Don"
22.12.2021

I'm Getting My Life Together
(Sto Mettendo Insieme la Mia Vita)

I'm making everything right.
I'm picking up the pieces.
I'm putting the jigsaw puzzle back together.
I'm remaking the picture...
...the picture of my life.
Because...
...I'm getting my life together.

It's been a while.
The picture wasn't clear.
The picture was broken up.
It was shattered into a million little pieces.
Now...
...I'm getting my life together.

It's about time.
The time has arrived.
The time is now.
There's not point wasting time.
There is no point in procrastinating.
The time has come and...
...I'm getting my life together.

"The Don"
26.12.2021

The End of Time

(La Fine dei Tempi)

It has been predicted.
It is not new.
When will it happen?
Are we getting close?
It seems that way.
Is this...
...the End of Time?

Probably not.
This is not new.
These times are not new.
It has seemed like this before.
The End of Time.

But, can I be sure?
Can you be sure?
Can anyone be sure?
This is not new.
These times are not new.
It has seemed like this before.
But...
...is this time different?
Is this really...
...the End of Time?

Maybe.
But probably not.

"The Don"
27.12.2021

Alive

(Viva)

Are you *breathing?*
Are you *walking?*
Are you *talking?*
Are you *listening?*
Are you *seeing?*
Are you *feeling?*
Are you *caring?*
Are you *hurting?*
Are you *suffering?*
Are you "Alive"?

Are you *awake?*
Are you *doing something?*
Are you gonna *give a helping hand?*
Are you gonna *lend you sister & brother a hand?*
Are you gonna *carry their burden for a while?*
Are you gonna *listen to their story?*
Are you gonna *hold them in your arms?*
Are you gonna *cry with them?*
Are you gonna *dry away their tears?*
Are you gonna *ease their suffering (just for a little while)?*

This is what it means to be "Alive"!

Are you "Alive"?

"The Don"
27.12.2021

The Youth Club

(Il Discoteca Giovanile)

This is a world for the youth.
Everything is directed at the youth.
The youth are the future.
Youth culture is what it's all about.
But what has happened to my youth?
Where did my youth go?
I am no longer a part of youth.
I do not belong to *"The Youth Club"!*

But...
...I am still a youth inside me.
And I think that I'm alright with that.
I'm ok.
I think that that's what matters most.
What's inside you.
And my youth is still inside me.
I haven't lost my youth.
My youth is still there.
Inside of me!
"And let's face it, that's what really counts!"
I still belong to "The Youth Club"!

"I am a YOUTH!"

"I am a permanent member of "The Youth Club"!"

Never let your membership to *"The Youth Club"* lapse.
For once lost, it's very hard, if not impossible, to rejoin!
Do NOT your *"Youth Club"* membership lapse...
...do NOT let it expire!

"The Don"
28.12.2021

Human Nature

(Natura Umana)

"It's just "Human Nature"!"
I hear this ALL the time?
"It's just "Human Nature"!"
WTF does this mean?
I have NO idea!
WTF is "Human Nature"?

Is *"Human Nature"* to be...
...*violent?*
...*cruel?*
...*uncaring?*
...*unkind?*
...*unfriendly?*
...*uncompassionate?*
...*selfish?*
...*suspicious?*
...*insensitive?*
...*inhuman?*
...*inhumane?*

Or is *"Human Nature"*...
...*peaceful?*
...*LO♥ING?*
...*caring?*
...*kind?*
...*friendly?*
...*compassionate?*
...*sharing?*
...*accepting??*
...*sensitive?*
...*human?*
...*humane?*

Is this "Human Nature"?

"The Don"
28.12.2021

Books written by "The Don"

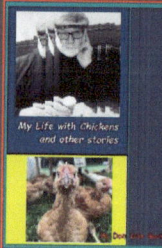

"My Life with Chickens & other stories: I Pity the Poor Immigrant"
Published:
10th September, 2019
*Autobiography Book 1:
0 – 12 years old*

"Poems for Misfits, Miscreants, Misanthropes, Mavericks, Losers & Malcontents!"
Published:
10th June, 2020
Book of Poems 1

"Poems for Troubled Minds & Trouble Hearts"
Published:
10th August, 2020
Book of Poems 2

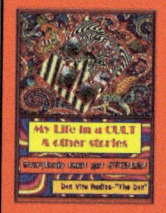

"My Life in a CULT & other stories: Everybody Must Get STONED!"
Published:
10th September, 2020
*Autobiography Book 2:
15 – 30 years old*

"Poems for Restless Minds & Restless Hearts"
Published:
10th October, 2020
Book of Poems 3

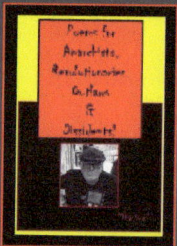

"Poems for Anarchists, Revolutionaries, Outlaws & Dissidents!"
Published:
10th November, 2020
Book of Poems 4

"Poems for Non-Thinkers & Eccentrics"
Published:
10th December, 2020
Book of Poems 5

"The Rantings of a Madman"
Published:
10th January, 2021
Book of Poems 6

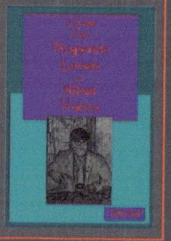

"Poems for Desperate Lovers & Silent Voices"
Published:
10th February, 2021
Book of Poems 7

"Poems for Tormented Minds & Tortured Souls"
Published:
10th March, 2021
Book of Poems 8

All available ONLY online

Books written by "The Don"

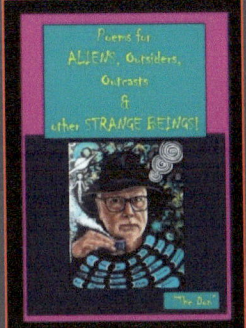

"Poems for ALIENS, Outsiders, Outcasts & other STRANGE BEINGS!"
Published: 10th April, 2021
Book of Poems 9

"Poems for Beings From Another Planet"
Published: 10th May, 2021
Book of Poems 10

"Poems for Mindless Beings & Lost Souls"
Published: 10th June, 2021
Book of Poems 11

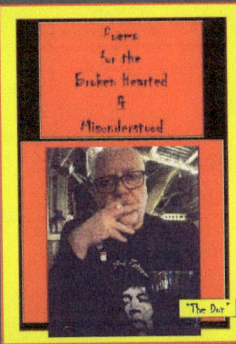

"Poems for the Broken Hearted & Misunderstood
Published: 10th July, 2021
Book of Poems 12

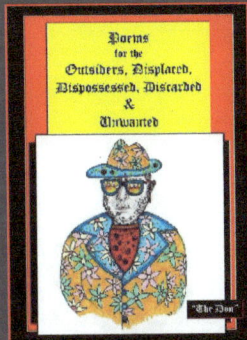

"Poems for Poems for the Bewildered, Dazed & Confused"
10th August, 2021

Book of Poems 13

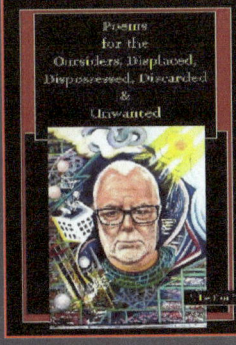

"Poems for the Outsiders, Displaced, Dispossessed, Discarded & Unwanted"
Published: 10th Sept, 2021
Book of Poems 14

All available ONLY online

"Poems for Secret Agents, Phantom Agents, Agents of Change, Agent Provocateurs & Agents of Chaos"
Published: 10th Oct, 2021
Book of Poems 15

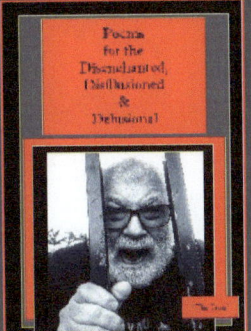

"Poems for Disenchanted, Disillusioned & Delusional"
Published: 10th November, 2021
Book of Poems 16

Books written by "The Don"

"Poems for the Stoners, drugos, ACID takers & Psychedelic LO❤ERS (Everybody Must Get Stoned)"
Published: 10th December, 2021
Book of Poems 17

"Poems for Anarchists, Rebels & Revolutionaries
Published: 10th January, 2022
Book of Poems 18

"Poems for Rebels, Radicals & Revolutionaries (Viva la Révolution!)"
Published: 10th February, 2022
Book of Poems 19

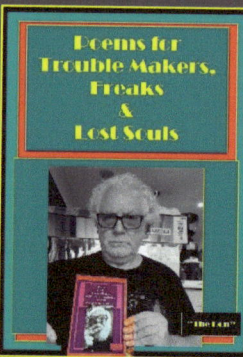

"Poems for Trouble Makers, Freaks & Lost Souls"
Published: 10th March 2022
Book of Poems 20

"Poems for Zombies & the Walking Dead"
Published: 10th April 2022
Book of Poems 21

Vito Radice ("The Don")
(Poet/Author/Polemicist/Non-Thinker/Non-Intellectual)
Email:
vitoradice@gmail.com
Instagram: don_vito_radice
Facebook: Vito Radice
Mobile: +61490012461
(Australia)

www.ingramcontent.com/pod-product-compliance
Lightning Source LLC
Chambersburg PA
CBHW042048290426
44109CB00006B/152